MW01109577

thank
you

You have made a difference in our business.
Thank you for your confidence in us.

Share these other Thank You books:

Thank You for Being There; Thank You for Being You;
Thank You, Friend; Thank You, Mom;
Thank You, Sister; Thank You for Your Thoughtfulness

Thank You for Your Business © 2004 by Howard Publishing Company
All rights reserved. Printed in the United States of America

Published by Howard Publishing Co., Inc.
3117 North 7th Street, West Monroe, Louisiana 71291-2227
www.howardpublishing.com

04 05 06 07 08 09 10 11 12 13   10 9 8 7 6 5 4 3 2 1

Written by Linda M. Wall
Edited by Between the Lines
Interior design by LinDee Loveland and Stephanie D. Walker

ISBN: 1-58229-369-4

thank you

for your

business

a collection of stories, quotes, and
encouragement to say thank you

HOWARD
®PUBLISHING CO.

thank you

You are the plumb line
by which we measure
our success. If you're
satisfied, we know we've
been true to our goal.

thank
you

Dear friend,

In this crazy, get-ahead world of business, it's easy to lose sight of what—or who—matters most. Making the numbers add up and keeping that competitive edge can seem more important than relationships.

But we know it's people that make a business successful. People like you.

You are important to us, much more than an account number or name on a file. You're the reason we dream and plan and work. It's you who keep us moving forward, always striving to give and to be our best.

So, thank you for your business. It's our great privilege to serve you, and we promise to continue to treat you—and your business—with the utmost care.

thank
you

Leadership
is a combination
of strategy and
character. If you
must be without
one, be without
the strategy.

GEN. H. NORMAN SCHWARZKOPF

thank you

You've helped make us
what we are:
a business with your needs
at heart. Thank you for
allowing us to serve you.

Investing in People

Patrons crowded the downtown bank, each vying for a turn at the teller window. If not for the balloons and streamers, it might have resembled an old-fashioned run on the bank.

The customers, bearing cards and flowers, waited to pay tribute to retiring teller Kendra Adams. A bank employee for three decades, Adams is known for disbursing not only funds but care as well.

"Kendra remembers everyone's name," one customer said. "She knows who's had a baby and who's out of work. She makes everybody feel important."

The branch manager said Adams personifies the bank's slogan, "Investing in People." Taking in the throng of well-wishers, he added, "What we're seeing here today is a return on that investment."

TEN WAYS TO BUILD
HEALTHY CUSTOMER RELATIONS

1. Keep your eye on the big picture, but don't overlook the details.

2. Do what's expected—then do more.

3. Promise only what you can give, and give what you promise.

4. Be honest and fair.

5. If you make a mistake, fix it—don't cover it up.

Build Healthy

6. Listen, listen, listen!

7. Deliver on time—or sooner.

8. Be available and approachable.

9. Let your customers know you value their business.

10. Treat each customer like the first one you ever had.

Customer Relations

Do not merely look out for your own personal interests, but also for the interests of others.

Philippians 2:4

NASB

Making a Difference

Marguerite Kline calls her health-insurance company her lifesaver—and she means that literally.

The sixty-nine-year-old grandmother of three suffered a heart attack while meeting recently with her insurance agent. Thanks to the company's Better Employee Program, the agent had just completed a CPR training course. Her efforts kept Kline alive while paramedics were en route.

The insurance company is one of many corporations offering its employees extracurricular class options ranging from stress-reduction techniques to martial arts. The classes are free, and employees who participate earn points toward bonuses or time off.

The idea, according to a company spokesperson, is to help people become healthier, happier individuals and employees. "The program is having a tremendous impact on people," he said.

Marguerite Kline couldn't agree more.

thank
you

Try not to become a man of success, but rather try to become a man of value.

ALBERT EINSTEIN

thank you

We have a lot in common:
you expect the best, and
we expect to give it.
Thanks for setting
the bar high.

Quality Trumps Quantity

Five years ago a small, regional replacement window company struggled to gain market share in an industry dominated by bigger and more widely recognized names. Recently that same company, still small by industry standards, swept past its competition to win a prestigious award for product excellence.

"We wouldn't have this award," the company's president said, "if we were still trying to grow at twice the industry pace." He said early efforts to achieve growth too quickly threatened to diminish the quality of their product.

"That's when we decided to forget leading-edge growth to focus on excellence instead."

The award recognized the commitment to excellence and affirmed what this company's president told his employees all along: "Bigger isn't always better."

Ten Tips for Boosting Employee Morale

1. Catch your employees doing something good—and let them know.

2. Celebrate successes.

3. Ask for feedback—and listen to it.

4. Include employees in decision making and planning.

5. Be constructive in your criticism.

6. Provide employees with the tools and the authority to do the job.

7. Assume nothing; communicate everything.

8. Remember your employees are people, not positions.

9. Keep your office door open.

10. Don't forget to build in a little fun.

Employee Morale

Work with a smile on your face, always keeping in mind that no matter who happens to be giving the orders, you're really serving God.

Ephesians 6:7

MSG

Personal Delivery

Shipping manager Elizabeth Halsey hates to be late. So her coworkers weren't surprised when a delivery truck broke down and Halsey loaded a shipment of computer parts into her own vehicle.

"All our other trucks were already dispatched," Halsey said. "I knew if we were going to deliver on time, we needed an alternative." The alternative was the backseat of Halsey's Toyota Camry.

Halsey not only delivered the shipment on schedule; she helped unload it. The unusual service didn't go unnoticed by staff at the receiving company.

"We were impressed," said the company's owner. "Elizabeth definitely went above and beyond."

Halsey didn't hang around to accept kudos. She was due at a staff meeting, and as already mentioned, she hates to be late.

They may forget
what you said,
but they will
never forget
how you made
them feel.

CARL W. BUECHNER

thank you

Your satisfaction is
at the top of our to-do list.
Thank you for being a
constant reminder
of what we're all about.

Landing
the Big Account

The creative team for an up-and-coming media company invested countless hours devising ways to win the coveted big account for which every company in town was vying. Suggestions included everything from high-tech presentations to corporate giveaways and expensive dinners.

The dedicated team eventually secured the account but, to its surprise, carefully planned strategies were not what sealed the deal.

"Lots of companies try to lure us with freebies and special handling," the owner of the much-courted company said. "Those things don't really impress me." What did catch his attention, he explained, was the simple art of listening.

"This team really *listened*. Other companies had showier presentations and slicker gimmicks, but I wanted someone who would hear me and what I want. We picked the company that did that."

A Great Boss . . .

1. Thinks before speaking.

2. Keeps cool even when things get hot.

3. Considers opposing points of view.

4. Is enthusiastic.

5. Listens.

6. Leads by example.

7. Treats employees with respect.

8. Defines and clearly communicates expectations.

9. Recognizes and rewards achievement.

10. Doesn't shoot the messenger!

A Great Boss . . .

In everything,
do to others what you
would have them do to you.

Matthew 7:12

NIV

The Christmas Gift

A cash-strapped elementary school recently took possession of a new copy machine and one hundred books for its library—compliments of a nearby office-equipment company.

The company was gearing up for its annual employee Christmas party when a member of the repair team, Harlan Anderson, mentioned the dilapidated condition of the school's equipment.

"Many of us have had children in that school at one time or another," Anderson said. "We wanted to help."

The staff voted unanimously to skip the annual party and apply the money toward a state-of-the-art copier for the school. Moved by its employees' generosity, the company's executives joined in with an additional gift of books for the school library.

"Helping someone else felt great," Anderson said. "And we had a great Christmas potluck instead."

It is not fair
to ask of others
what you are not
willing to do
yourself.

ELEANOR ROOSEVELT

thank you

In a world of endless options, we're grateful you chose us. We appreciate you and your business.

Safer Skies

Thanks to the creativity of one flight attendant, select passengers on a growing discount airline can enjoy in-flight movies for free—and help make air travel safer at the same time.

The flight attendant, concerned with passenger inattention to in-flight safety instructions, offered a solution that won first prize in her airline's Safer Skies employee contest. Her winning entry suggested that passengers seated near emergency exits be issued free headphones in exchange for viewing a brief video presentation on safety.

"Targeting passengers in key seating areas helps drive home the importance of their roles, plus the free headphones give the added benefit of access to the in-flight movie," the forward-thinking employee explained.

The airline's president praised the attendant's innovative thinking, saying, "Sometimes the best ideas come from the people closest to the situation."

Ten Business Principles from the Book of Proverbs

1. Commit your work to God.
Commit to the LORD
whatever you do, and your plans will succeed.
—Proverbs 16:3 NIV

2. Employ fair business practices.
The LORD detests differing weights,
and dishonest scales do not please him.
—Proverbs 20:23 NIV

3. Work hard.
Lazy hands make a man poor,
but diligent hands bring wealth.
—Proverbs 10:4 NIV

4. Plan ahead.
He who gathers crops in summer is a wise son,
but he who sleeps during harvest is a disgraceful son.
—Proverbs 10:5 NIV

5. Listen to sound counsel.
He who walks with the wise grows wise,
but a companion of fools suffers harm.
—Proverbs 13:20 NIV

Business

6. Speak up for the little guy.
Speak up for those who cannot speak for themselves,
for the rights of all who are destitute.
—Proverbs 31:8 NIV

7. Don't make wealth your only goal.
Do not wear yourself out to get rich;
have the wisdom to show restraint.
—Proverbs 23:4 NIV

8. Accept criticism.
He who listens to a life-giving rebuke
will be at home among the wise.
—Proverbs 15:31 NIV

9. Encourage those you lead.
A man finds joy in giving an apt reply—
and how good is a timely word!
—Proverbs 15:23 NIV

10. Exercise patience.
A patient man has great understanding,
but a quick-tempered man displays folly.
—Proverbs 14:29 NIV

Principles

Everyone should be
quick to listen,
slow to speak and slow to
become angry.

James 1:19

NIV

Have Search Engine, Will Travel

A midsized software company recently sent a dozen of its technicians packing. It wasn't a case of corporate downsizing but rather a groundbreaking initiative aimed at bolstering use of the company's latest Web-search software.

The crew of technicians was dispatched to existing customers to provide free, on-site upgrading for newly reconstructed search engines. The goal was to make the switch to the updated software consumer-friendly while encouraging sales of related products.

The bold move proved successful. An astounding 65 percent of customers opted for the upgrade, compared with 20 percent before the on-site service. In addition, a number of new products were sold.

"We chose to go the extra mile—literally," the company's chief of technology said, "and our customers appreciate it."

thank
you

You get the best
out of others
when you give
the best
of yourself.

HARRY FIRESTONE

thank you

God has blessed our
business with faithful
clients like you. We'll work
hard to keep earning your
loyalty and trust.

From Panhandlers
to Promoters

The owner of an urban restaurant knew he had a problem when customers began complaining about street people begging for change. Many patrons were annoyed by the confrontations and stopped coming to the restaurant.

His managers tried without success to discourage the panhandlers. "Most were homeless teens," the owner explained, "hungry and with nowhere else to go."

Then it hit him. Instead of running them off, why not put the kids to work?

So he equipped willing teens with fliers and sandwich boards, promising them minimum wage and a hot meal in exchange for promoting the restaurant during peak hours.

"It's great," the restaurateur said. "My customers are happy, and fewer kids will go to sleep hungry tonight."

TEN WAYS TO BEAT JOB STRESS

1. Do something physical—take up kick boxing, go jogging, or ride a bike.

2. Take good care of yourself—get enough sleep, eat healthy meals, exercise.

3. Spend time with people you love.

4. Do something you enjoy—if you don't have a hobby, get one.

5. Escape from the routine—take a vacation, read a good book, go for a walk.

6. Reward yourself when you come to the end of a hard day or a tough project.

7. Find a confidant—someone who'll listen without judgment.

8. Laugh often.

9. Keep things in perspective, and don't forget to breathe.

10. Give each day and each circumstance to God.

Beat Job Stress

Let us not become weary
in doing good, for at the
proper time we will
reap a harvest if
we do not give up.

Galatians 6:9

NIV

Saving
the Company

An undercapitalized manufacturing company desperately needed to get its new product into distribution. A major equipment failure in the eleventh hour, however, appeared to be the last straw for the struggling company.

Owner Martin Jackson knew this would mean the demise of his business—and the layoff of his thirty-two loyal employees. After years of working to expand operations and risking everything on a new product line, he would have to shut the company down.

But the staff wasn't interested in giving up.

Not a single worker went home that night. Every employee, without directive from the boss, stayed on the job until the equipment was repaired and production was rolling once more.

Years later employees still tell the story of the night they saved the company.

Success
seems to be largely
a matter of
hanging on after
others have let go.

WILLIAM FEATHER